The Legacy

_____

Insert loved one's name above

_____

Age at time of interview

_____

Date of interview

What people are saying about Forever Legacy Book

"Time doesn't stop for anyone. If you have a loved one and you want to remember their story or share their wisdom (and jokes) with generations to come, this book is great. Even if you're too busy now to create a video or transfer the text and photos to a digital book, you'll have the answers all ready to go when you do have time. I think this book is an excellent buy for anyone who wants to preserve their family's legacy." -Elizabeth S.

"Forever Legacy is one of the most amazing gifts you can give. And it's not just a gift to your family, but to yourself. The book guides you through the steps of a personal interview with a loved one. You will learn so much about them—their origins, their story, the wisdom they've acquired in their life journey—and it can be recorded for posterity so that even the youngest members of your family can come to know them. It's such a simple, but powerful idea." -Jerry B.

"I can't say enough about what a treasure this book will truly be for our family. To have a convenient and guided format to record intimate and cherished memories is a genuine gift that will be enjoyed for generations." -Kelly G.

Printed in the United States of America

First Printing, 2019

ISBN 9781791564636

Jeff Underwood DBA Mission Media
3672 Georgia Street #C3
San Diego, CA 92103

www.ForeverLegacyBook.com

forever

LEGACY BOOK

This is dedicated to you, Mom

Special thanks goes out to a great many people, without whom this book may have never been possible:

Alex Tiscareno	Kelly George
Amie Brown	Kendra Losee
Belinda Donner	Kent Koopman
Bette Gourley	Kim Blake
Charles Reidelbach	Laura Torres
Craig Caston	Laurie Zagon
Dan Wilkinson	Lavonne Woodbridge
Danny Jones	Marlene Sanchez
Dave Gibbs	Mary Beth Caston
Don Lewis	Matthew Rivaldi
Dr. Kamlesh Mehta	Mike Scappechio
DLA Piper	Ngozi Agbo
Eva Starr	Phillip Elgie
Janice Watson	Rachel Maguire
Jason Bell	Rich Brocchini
Jean Seley	Rick Watson
Jeanette Arango	Sandy Hendren
Jeff Hall	Siobhan Blume
Jerry Burkey	Tony Moore
Joe Sorrentino	Zoe

Introduction

There are no guarantees for how much time we have with the people we love.

After starting a service in 2017 to help everyday people produce professional legacy videos for their families, I decided to make it even easier and more affordable so that anyone could preserve their family members' most essential life lessons. This book will walk you through the process of my job, being the interviewer and documentarian of your loved one's legacy. As this book helps their story unfold, you will learn more about your loved one, and also, how their story helps you to better understand yourself and your roots.

Giving this book is much more than a traditional gift. You will be giving your undivided attention while you sit down and get to know your loved one on a deeper level; and while making a family keepsake in the process. Please keep in mind: this is not a blank journal you give to your loved one, hoping they will fill it out on their own. This is an opportunity to sit down and fill in the pages together as your loved one shares their most cherished stories and life lessons with you.

It felt so good for me to make legacy videos for my family. I firmly believe that you, too, will find this experience to be rewarding and, better yet, fun!

May this be only the beginning of an inspiring journey of giving the things that truly matter: your time, your attention, and the gift of forever.

Happy sharing!

How to use this book

What you hold in your hands may quite possibly become your family's most prized possession. Within these pages will soon contain the history and legacy of your family story. And if you are interviewing a dear friend, you are giving them the gift of preserving their family story for them! To make this gift a surprise for your loved one, you might want to tell them that you need to interview them for a special work project or a child's class project.

Please keep in mind that—instead of giving your loved one this book as a blank journal for them to complete on their own—Forever Legacy Book is meant to be an experience for you both to share together. When you're finished, I have a feeling that conducting the interview will have been one of the best parts of the experience. And it will also make you the living, breathing historian who will help carry on your loved one's legacy. You will soon be the expert when it comes to their story and life lessons. Furthermore, instead of putting the burden on your loved one to complete these questions as just one more thing on their to-do list, give them the gift of your time to use the book as a reason to spend quality time together. As a child, I always wished I had a grown-up relationship with my grandparents (and seniors in general) so we could have deep, "adult" conversations and share wisdom with one another. With that in mind, here's how you can get the most from this book.

1. Start Recording

I highly recommend that you use an audio or video recording app on your phone to capture the interview so you have it archived for the future. If your interview is not paired with a professional video shoot and you think your loved one might be camera-shy, you could set up the camera on a tripod next to you. Or

START AN AUDIO OR VIDEO RECORDER

you can set it up in front of you so your loved one is looking "through" the camera as they answer your questions, which is how I like to record my legacy video interviews. I like to think about how when the subject is speaking to the camera, they will someday be speaking directly to someone from a future generation who is watching their legacy video. To ensure the best quality recording, I recommend that you choose a location that will be relatively quiet or add a microphone attachment to your recording device. If recording video, be mindful to choose flattering lighting for your loved one. When I'm traveling for a legacy video shoot and won't have studio lights with me, I try to position my subject so they are facing natural light from a window with sheer curtains to diffuse the light. Or I choose a window that is far enough away so the sunlight is not falling directly on my subject's face. If you are conducting your interview outdoors, position your loved one in the shade so you can achieve the same effect of diffused light as you would with a window with sheer curtains.

2. Interview

Next, go through the questions in the book, which start at page 10. To help keep both your and your loved ones energy levels up, I suggest only tackling one section at a time. So, for your first visit, ask all the questions of the Childhood section; for the next visit, move on to Adolescence; and so on until you've completed all four sections. You could take

notes in the book during the interview, but I would actually recommend focusing your undivided attention on the conversation instead. And when the interview has finished, you will be able to go back through the audio (or the video) you recorded and transcribe the interview into the pages of the book. By saving the writing part until later, you will free yourself up to enjoy the quality time with your loved one.

3. Select Photos

For almost every question page, there is a corresponding photo page to add one or more visuals to enhance the question even more. For these photo pages, we recommend that you scan or take a digital photo of the archival photo you find from a photo album. That way, you won't damage or lose one of the historical

photos AND you'll have a digital file which you can label "Childhood1, Childhood2, Childhood3, etc." to match up with each question from this book. And instead of attaching the original photo to the photo pages of this book, I recommend printing out a copy, which will be thinner and reduce the risk of a precious photo falling out by accident. Once you have the photos selected and organized with file names, it will be a breeze to edit together a legacy video down the road. If you have trouble finding a photo for a particular question, try doing a search on Google Images. Just go to www.images. google.com, type in some descriptive text into the search bar, and then select Tools > Usage rights > "Labeled for reuse." By using this filter, you'll know that the photo you've selected will not pose any copyright issues if you decide to create a video later to share online. A couple other handy websites for royalty-free photos are www.unsplash.com and www.pixabay.com.

4. Transcribe the Audio and Edit Legacy Videos

If you have a busy life and the task of transcribing all that audio makes you sweat a little, I have a solution for you. Hire a service to do the heavy lifting. Companies like www. rev.com charge $1.00 per minute of audio to transcribe it for you. Once it's been transcribed, you can write it into the pages of the book, confident that you didn't miss anything like you would if you tried writing it all down during the interview. And if you run out of space, make a note that the story is continued on a page number from the "Additional Notes" section in the back of the book. When editing each of your loved one's responses into a short legacy video, highlight the best parts of their story and combine it with the photo(s) that you collected together. Most computers already come with video editing software. If not, there's plenty of free editing software you can download. There's even video editing apps that can be downloaded directly to your smartphone or tablet. Cut your clips down to about 3 minutes or less if possible, add music, add photos, and if you have the information to include, add captions to explain each photo when it appears on screen.

After the book has been filled out, this will make a priceless keepsake, but what if it just sits on the shelf, and your loved one's friends, family, and younger generations never hear the story for themselves? Capturing each response into a legacy video is another way to preserve the story, share it easily on social media, and appeal to younger audiences. This is a way to honor your loved one right now and not wait until the unfortunate event of a funeral for others to get to know them on a deeper level.

Once the book has been filled out and photos attached, present your gift as part of a special event for your loved one's birthday. As an added surprise, you could invite him or her to a local library or bookstore to attend a book reading for fun. Imagine your loved one arriving to find in the audience all of their closest friends and family members. Then, when the event is about to start, the host can announce that the book reading will be— surprise!— "The Legacy of [the name of your loved one]."

If you have any questions about how to use this book or produce your legacy videos, reach out to us on our social media accounts. Our homepage, **www.foreverlegacybook**. com has a link to all of them. When you post your behind-the-scenes moments or your finished Forever Legacy memories on social media, we would love to see what you came up with. Tag us with our handle **@foreverlegacybook** or our hashtag **#foreverlegacybook** and we might help you share it with the world. And after all, don't our loved ones deserve to be just as famous as all those reality TV stars?

Wishing you many more memories to come!

Sincerely,

Jeff Underwood

Help your loved one fill in their family tree

Get a glimpse of your roots. Write your full name and birthplace in the bottom circle, your parents' full names and birthplaces in the middle level, and your grandparents' names and birthplaces in the top level.

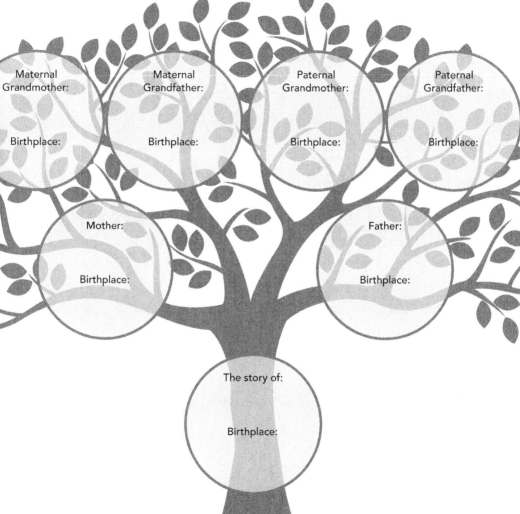

The interview starts here…

Childhood

Did you have a happy childhood? Or were there challenges you had to deal with at a young age?

Describe your childhood home: where was it, how big was it, what you loved most about it? How do you think the place you grew up helped shape you into who you are today?

_____

_____

_____

_____

_____

_____

Attach a photo of your childhood home here.

How did you like to play and have fun as a kid?
Do you feel like you're still in touch with that same playfulness and inner child today? If so, how?

_____

_____

_____

_____

_____

_____

Attach a photo of your favorite childhood toy.

What were your childhood chores? Were there any that you especially hated or maybe actually enjoyed?

_____

_____

_____

_____

_____

_____

Attach a photo of the room you were cleaning or a tool or appliance you used to complete your chores you describe on the opposite page.

What were your earliest pop culture influences? Which books, music albums, TV shows, and/or movies most stand out in your memory? What was it that you loved so much about it?

_____

_____

_____

_____

_____

_____

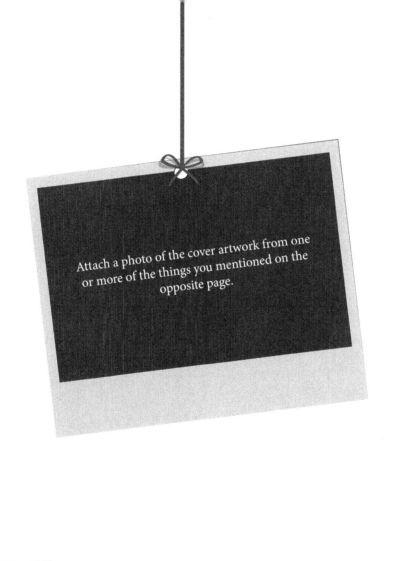

Attach a photo of the cover artwork from one or more of the things you mentioned on the opposite page.

Is there anything from your education that you feel has been especially important in preparing you for success later in life?

_____

_____

_____

_____

_____

_____

Adolescence

Looking back, was there anything in particular you
wanted to be when you grew up?
What was it about that job that appealed to you?

Who was your first childhood crush? Did you ever date or spend time together?

_____

_____

_____

_____

_____

_____

Attach a photo of your crush from that era.

What advice would you give to that younger version of yourself?

_____

_____

_____

_____

_____

_____

Attach a photo of yourself from your teenage years.

Was education important to you growing up? If so, what subjects do you feel helped you the most later in life? If not, where do you feel you gained the most wisdom about life?

_____

_____

_____

_____

_____

_____

Attach a photo of person you look up or from whom you have learned a great amount.

What was a major challenge you overcame during your young adult years? Did that experience teach you a valuable life lesson?

_____

_____

_____

_____

_____

_____

What was your first paying job? Were there any perks or challenges that came with that job? Did you have any creative ways of making money as a kid?

_____

_____

_____

_____

_____

_____

Attach a photo of yourself (or the location) from one of your earliest jobs.

Adulthood

Was there a specific moment from your past when you felt like you had reached adulthood?

What type of work did you pursue in your working years? How did you decide to follow that particular line of work?

_____

_____

_____

_____

_____

_____

Attach a photo that represents your career field.

Please describe one of the highlights you experienced
during your career.

_____

_____

_____

_____

_____

_____

Attach a photo of yourself at your job from your working years.

Did you marry or find a life partner? If so, how did you meet him or her? What attracted you to them?

_____

_____

_____

_____

_____

_____

Attach a photo of yourself with your partner.

Did you have kids? What advice would you give to people deciding whether or not to have kids?

_____

_____

_____

_____

_____

_____

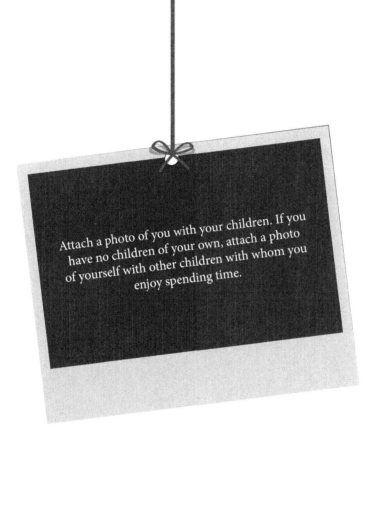

Attach a photo of you with your children. If you have no children of your own, attach a photo of yourself with other children with whom you enjoy spending time.

Throughout your life, what did you want the most? Is that thing that you toiled to attain throughout your working years still something you value today?

_____

_____

_____

_____

_____

_____

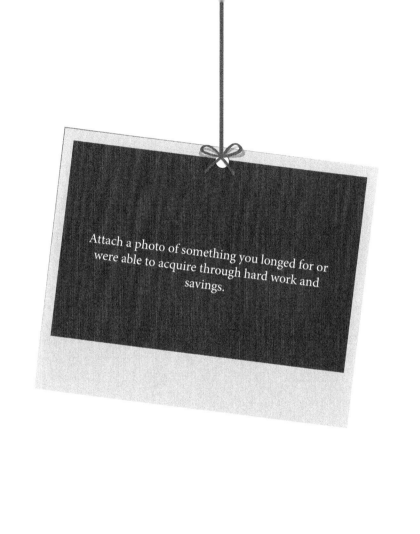

Attach a photo of something you longed for or were able to acquire through hard work and savings.

Golden Years

How does it feel to be in the golden years of your life?

When most people daydream about retirement, they imagine themselves traveling much more than they do now. Is there anywhere you've traveled where you'd love to return to? What was it about that place that stands out to you?

_____

_____

_____

_____

_____

_____

Attach a photo of yourself from that place.

Do you have any regrets up until this point in your life?

_____

_____

_____

_____

_____

_____

Attach a photo that represents the thing you'd like to do differently.

Is there a word of advice you could give younger generations that you think could help them?

_____

_____

_____

_____

_____

_____

Attach a photo of a person you look up to or from whom you have learned a great amount.

When your loved ones think back to their time spent with you, how do you hope to be remembered?

_____

_____

_____

_____

_____

_____

Attach a photo of you enjoying yourself.

For someone who is much younger and still trying to make it in the world, what are your 3 biggest life lessons you would share with them?

_____

_____

_____

_____

_____

_____

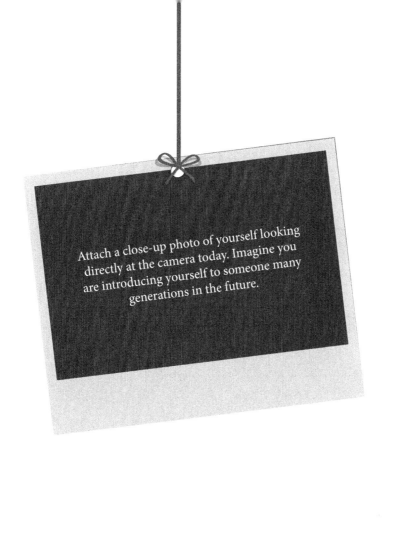

Attach a close-up photo of yourself looking directly at the camera today. Imagine you are introducing yourself to someone many generations in the future.

Printing copies of your legacy book

Congratulations on getting to this stage of the book! If you'd like to make more copies to give as gifts to family and friends, we recommend a custom printing service such as **www.apple.com/macos/print-products/** to have your loved one's stories and photos put into a high-quality photo book. If you're not working from an Apple computer/device, another option is **www.nationsphotolab.com/photobooks.aspx**. To upload the written content of your legacy book copies, you could retype your loved one's answers, or simply take a photo of the portion of the Forever Legacy Book page that contains the handwritten material.

Creating legacy videos

At this point, you have documented some of your loved one's biggest life lessons and curated a selection of photos to accompany each of those memories. The good news is that you have already finished the hard part needed to create one or more legacy videos. By taking the audio or video you recorded during your interview (or by shooting new footage), you can now take what you have captured in this book and elevate it to the next level by making a legacy video for each of the questions your loved one answered.

Most people struggle with what to give their parents during holidays, birthdays, and other special occasions. A "Do-It-Yourself" (DIY) legacy video might be just the thing to surprise Mom or Dad. A legacy video goes beyond a typical video biography by giving the viewer a quick glimpse of one of your loved one's most significant life lessons, all in about 3 minutes. These bite-sized videos are much easier to share via email and social media, helping younger generations connect more deeply with Grandma and Grandpa.

You can make a legacy video with the technology you probably already have. All that's needed is a smartphone. Legacy videos are a new concept that most people don't even consider, so not only will you save money on gift giving—you will get bonus points for originality, too! To give you an idea of what's possible, check out some samples at

www.foreverlegacyvideo.com/video-archive or at our Vimeo page at **www.vimeo. com/foreverlegacyvideo**. Similar to YouTube, Vimeo has an app you can download to your smartphone, tablet, or smart TV to play these legacy video samples from the convenience of your home using the ways you already enjoy viewing all your favorite media content.

To create a DIY legacy video from the stories you've captured in this book, here's a couple things to think about:

Editing your legacy videos

Most computers already come with video editing software. If not, a quick Google search will give you plenty of free and low-cost options you can download to your computer. There's even video editing apps that can be downloaded directly to your smartphone or tablet! Once you choose the software you want to edit your legacy video with, add a title at the beginning to give viewers a quick idea of what the story is about. Take the audio or video clips that relate to the title of your legacy video, and trim them down to about 3 minutes (or less if possible). During the interview, cut to the photo or photos that you pre-selected for this book to help the story appeal to a wider audience. Lastly, add music to your video. Just be sure the song is not distracting from the interview audio. And be sure to set the levels with your editing software low enough so that the music is not too loud to hear your interview.

Sharing your video(s)

We suggest uploading your finished legacy video directly to social media sites like Facebook, so family members around the world can enjoy them with you. To make this gift even more special, invite friends and family over for a Hollywood-themed screening party and hold a Q&A session afterward with the star of the show! To give your legacy videos even more exposure, please tag us in your Facebook post with our handle **@foreverlegacybook**. We'd love to see what you came up with!

For more helpful tips and links, go to **www.foreverlegacyvideo.com/diy**

Additional Notes

_____

_____

_____

_____

_____

_____

3 biggest lessons for your grandchilds
Page 29
How did you meet Lillian And Anne
How you

We would love to stay in touch! Join our online community, review this book, and download our free eBook.

facebook.com/
ForeverLegacyBook

Printed in Great Britain
by Amazon